In My Own Special Way
By Grace Oakley

First edition copyright © 2022 Grace Oakley

ISBN 13: 978-0-578-28348-7

All rights reserved. No part of this publication may be reproduced, stored in a retrieval system or transmitted in any form or by any means, electronic, mechanical, photocopying, recording or otherwise, without the prior written permission of the publisher and author.

Published by Grace Oakley, New Jersey
Design and layout by In My Own Special Way
Printed in the United States of America

In My Own Special Way
Building Self-Esteem in Children
This book demonstrates how children learn,
create, and explore freely in
their own special ways.

This book is dedicated to all of the children of the world. God made you special in His own special way.

BE GREAT!!

I am special in my own special way.

I can play with my pet in my own special way.

I can go to school in my own special way.

I can play the piano in my own special way.

I can play basketball in my own special way.

I can be a twin in my own special way.

I can love my brother in my own special way.

I can love my sister in my own special way.

I can play a guitar in my own special way.

I can run in my own special way.

I can be curious in my own special way.

I can smile in my own special way.

I can sleep in my own special way.

I can ride a horse in my own special way.

We can dress up in our own special way.

We are all special in our own special way.

Customer reviews

★★★★★ 5 out of 5
2 global ratings

Top reviews from the United States

 dermetric drye

★★★★★

Very good material

Reviewed in the United States on March 23, 2018

Great book to start your kids off with great confidence builder ...

One person found this helpful

Helpful   Report

 G

★★★★★

This books help children feel proud about themselves

Reviewed in the United States on April 12, 2022

I like this book because of the pictures and its a easy read for children.

★★★★★

Kimberly Darling · 8 hours ago

Great For Beginner Readers!

This book is great for beginner readers. Love that the illustrations are real pictures, very appealing to my daughter. You can tell the author knows what will attract children and appeal to young readers. Highly recommend and look forward to more work from this author!

✔ Yes, I recommend this product.

★★★★★

Anonymous · 4 years ago

Great Book! Easy To Read, Colorful Pages And A Wonderful Message E ...

Great book! Easy to read, colorful pages and a wonderful message enforcing that everyone is special and unique. Highly recommended.

★★★★★

Lisa53 · 2 years ago

A Very Excellent Read!

This book is a excellent read for children who are beginner readers. As you read "In My Own Special Way", along with your child, you'll get a sense of relief being that Grace M Oakley book/pages are not long to read. Her book is literally 10 pages of reading and children who are beginner readers can learn to read her very simple book/read. Grace M Oakley, I appreciate this book to the fullest. I rate this book 5 Stars, and if I could've rate it higher, I sure would have. I recommend any parents who child is a beginner readers, to purchase " Grace M Oakley book, In My Own Special Way"!

🏷 Tags: Great for Gifting

✔ Yes, I recommend this product.

★★★★★

beget · 8 hours ago

In My Own Special Way

This book is a great read for children learning how to read

✔ Yes, I recommend this product.

★★★★★

Lillian Pryor · 19 hours ago

Great Children's Book

I bought this book for my grandson. It is a wonderful way for children to learn self esteem and how to respect others!

SOCIAL MEDIA

www.ingramcontent.com/pod-product-compliance
Lightning Source LLC
LaVergne TN
LVHW072103070426
835508LV00002B/252